CHOKECHERRY HUNTERS AND OTHER POEMS

FOREWORD BY FRANK WATERS
BY JOSEPH L. CONCHA

THE SUNSTONE PRESS
Santa Fe, New Mexico

Copyright © 1976 by Joseph L Concha

ALL RIGHTS RESERVED

ISBN 0 - 913270 - 57 - 1

Acknowledgements

Special thanks to Ruth Hatcher and Dick Spas, who contributed their talents generously to make this book possible.

WOODCUTS ON COVER AND PAGE 5 BY ALEX CONCHA

Manufactured in the United States of America

FOREWORD
By
Frank Waters

In 1969 the first collection of poems by Joseph L. Concha, a fifteen year old Indian boy of Taos Pueblo, was published under the title Lonely Deer. The sensitive perception of these early verses was first recognized by the late, great art teacher at the Pueblo school, Stan Aiello, who raised money from private donors to subsidize the publication. Their faith was confirmed when the small book proved to be immensely popular.

Most of the verses reflected a child's response to nature: the first snow, twilight on the prairie, dark of the desert, winter footprints. Yet they all carried an undertone of sadness, of the transiency of life, unusual to a young boy, as so well expressed in the short title poem:
Lonely are the deer
the only hearts
filled with everlasting sorrow
and sadness
Hopes of tomorrow
are gone with the wind
Can he last for long?

It was this quality that immediately impressed me, for it is the same brooding vision imbuing the great lyrical poetry of the ancient Nahua peoples of Mexico, the Aztecs and the Toltec poet-king Nezahualcoyotl.

Joseph Concha, now twenty-one years old, presents here his second collection of poems. He has been away to the university, he is maturing. Joyfully he returns to his home pueblo and mountains. The appeal is still strong from leaf, clouds, summer rains, and chokecherry hunters. But everything is not quite the same.

*A leaf floats downstream
upon its last dream
not able to fly . . .*

*

*Grandfather's field
is already plowed
and I seem to taste
the sadness of a Grandmother
I never met*

He has had many new experiences, including peach wine; his face was drunk, "lying in a coffin of smoke, a whitehouse of feelings," knowing that "tomorrow I shall be alone, sitting on the edge of my prayers."
And again:
  *. . . In this darkness
    I don't belong . . .*
But this concisely written short book does not suggest that "You Can't Go Home Again." For we, like Joseph, can go home again; we are always going home again – not in linear time, but in a spiral from whose upper levels we see in different perspectives gained from our ever-maturing experiences.

And what is our heart's home but the eventual, universal, spiritual heartland from which we are temporarily alienated during our transient physical stays on our earthland?

It would be a great disservice should I foolishly attempt to sound the meanings of these heartfelt poems. They must be read by each reader for himself – and often twice. But my own feeling is that Joseph Concha, through childhood and youth, is recording the steps of his way toward that wholeness of spiritual maturity that sometime must be achieved by us all.

* * * *

RED WILLOW

I. Coming back
When women plaster the houses
and most of the young people
in school; some far-away place . . .

II. Others went to Jicarilla
and its quiet, like beyond the foggy
mountains in the mornings
there's only old people, dogs and
those who chase the lady in the
red skirt . . .

III. My thoughts are on sweet corn
and a new house
not wondering about older brothers
but when mushroom afternoons come.

I kick a rock
and see a dog
running after a car.

9/15/74

Deer mother
you sat at the head
of the valley
like a beautiful song
your image came to me
without wind
the corn pollen
lay at your feet
the fur on your back
was like a dream
looking at me
in the dawn of winter
the warmth of your womb
sent clouds of steam
towards my heart
that left me
feeling like a lover . . .

OH SWEET HER

beneath a forgotten pine tree
a drum echos
and the songs fade into the rain
it is the last dance
before morning

a dozen hearts away from me
somewhere nervous eyes lurk
waiting to be picked up
dancing nearer and nearer

fog creeps down the valley
and i must stop
before my mind wanders
over to her camp
because she never had long hair . . .

Grandmother
before i learned to crawl
you turned golden
like an aspen leaf
and flew away
from my open arms . . .

an experience
my hands become shapeless
amidst thunder beings
and lizards . . .

hot water and emotions
turned to dust . . .

deep red canyons
in time . . .

a young man sings
about death . . .

I am falling down
because I am too proud
I am watching myself
because I am crazy
you would be glad
my life will be gone
drained out of my body
to flow all over the universe
I will wish then
I could cry like a newborn baby . . .

FROM A RAINDROP

Wet daffodils and dark skies
filled my stomach
as grounded blackbirds weep
evaporating into loneliness
and twenty-five dollar summers
laying in a sea of mud
as my paranoid feet
sneaked over them . . .

the skies were full of grey clouds
my mind was hurting
the rain began to fall
too late to run
I walked away with a heavy heart
because the cold, muddy road
led nowhere . . .

a seemingly unending windstorm
displays itself with untouched fury
hovering over a holy sun
killing all the shadows and
tormenting the tall trees . . .

three hours of rain
looking at the sky
wishing i could cry
the midnight train
just brought pain
don't leave me behind
don't cut the line
three hours of rain . . .

'74

Summer rains
on the other side
of the mountain
and my dreams stretch
like a rainbow . . .

down, down, down
a breeze so cool
the rich aroma of the earth
comes to an end . . .

                                      9/8/71

Clouds,
give me your shadows
now that the sun
has burned my body . . .

CHOKECHERRY HUNTERS

a new morning
among the drifting cotton
the chokecherry hunters sing . . .

spoon mountains
          in a rainstorm

thunderflash
          end of rainstorm

under the stars
          a sweet smell
                    leaves out thoughts.

AUGUST

Drifting across the Taos mountains
early morning fog blankets

the crying horses
a call to memories

a drum beats by the creek
stirring anxious hearts in rhythm . . .

LEAF

a leaf floats downstream
upon its last dream
not able to fly . . .

Alone
on a hill
the wind blows
and you came like a dream . . .

holy sun, full of light
the moon is with you
blessed art thou among nature
and blessed is our way of life
holy earth, mother of gods
hear our songs
now and at the four corners . . .

Grandfather's field
is already plowed
and I seem to taste
the sadness of a Grandmother
I never met

In the valley
I stood
looking at your face
in beauty . . .

Here I am without fear, looking towards a mountain
in the distance
tomorrow night can wait till some other time,
a bald peak looms below the clouds
and beneath it a lost paradise
golden corn fields lay in the shadows,
as the secret of the hill flutters
about in the afternoon
like a restless butterfly,
a day to be remembered perhaps.

                            sitting alone
                            among stars and
                            cold mornings
                            last nights leave me blind
                            thinking of hot springs
                            wanting to try peach wine
                            but afraid to leave my mountain
                            my shadow cries for you . . .

The throbbling of my head and arms
looking out of a roofless house
at jumping night creatures
escaping into trees

screaming silently in my mind
messages of despair look back
towards bright signs

seconds are lost in one turn
like aspirin
waiting to save me . . .

AND

The
Tumbleweedisstuck
along a fence
the sun
rides the sky
like a 747 jumbo jet
watching brushfires
till 3:30 am
broken heart
divorce on a bike
a killer with an axe
I shall wake up late and . . .

HE could have walked
a dozen paths
if death had not
pursued

the dog stares
into its own thoughts
puppies' dreams
and god to superman . . .

Hear me stars
upon this dark night
just as the sacred mountain
which rises above my eyes
are my thoughts
as sweet as the plum blossom scent
and water from an irrigation ditch

in this darkness
I don't belong . . .

I am stuck deep
in a dark cloud
a sinking feeling
desperate hands reach out
a half-million tears
pushing me towards a shore
in early morning waves . . .

black, black, black,
strangled by the clouds,
the sun dies

thousands of upset
stomachs
thousands of snowflakes
falling
bleeding my courage
swallowing my thoughts

left and right
the bell begins to toll,
on my way to gamble
at the community house . . .

I NEED YOU IN THE NIGHT POEM

A purple haze filled the room
drifting among the black lights
and people who never got old
sat among us
clouds of
smoke
bells
ringing
in my ears
like organ music in waves
ha, ha, ha, ha, . . .

my face was drunk
lying in a coffin of smoke
a whitehouse of feelings

tomorrow
I shall be alone
sitting on the edge of my prayers

One sunrise
with spilled coffee
like abandoned birds nest
along an irrigation ditch
her name comes to me
my afternoon's gone . . .

eyeshadows
seem to betray me
i don't know why
i would rather by barefoot
in a grassy meadow
wet with melting snow . . .

The air bubbles in my tortilla
get Bigger
going down the highway
at sundown
wrapped in a blanket
thinking of ideas
which leave me drunk . . .

When the leaves fall
shall I sing my own song
beside the glowing fire
sending my voice against darkness

fighting cold mornings
and steep mountain trails
sleeping beside streams
going nowhere

draining forty years of death
from shadows and rocks
streaming into the valley . . .

if i could see autumn before you,
my eyes would never look back,
at the beauty falling at my feet

a moonlit valley
where the elk could be heard
but be nowhere in sight

and hunters slept lightly
then for a moment
did i see you run away with my youth . . .

play the happiest song,
read the poem i never wrote,
and catch the feeling
i felt yesterday
it was as big as a mountain,
full of deer trails

and try to be a man
firing a gun
to let your brother know
where you are
when he is on the
other side of the valley . . .

Eight dollar mr. america shoes,
floating in warm rain water
it's no fun being wet

but it's better than sleeping

next to a dead cat
a thousand times before sunday afternoons
wished i was thinking of home
instead of last night . . .

                                          6/17/72

           my heart is burning
           and the waves turn
           in the sea of my feelings
           the nausea of movement
           did i walk on water?

beautiful dreams
the hurt still hurts
empty highways
going nowhere
my luck would be better
if i don't play hero
not a dream
just sleep i hope

why do i think of running . . . ?

                        Have you gone so far
                        that i cry
                        because you cannot hear . . .

The Sun
Slowly sank
from the winter sky
little dirt's heart quivered
the valley seemed to fill up
once of a lifetime
strong-hearted songs
were far as the morning star
some winds sang some songs
the moon appeared in the sky.

12/30/72

to be one of them
and sway in the wind
like a blue spruce
whose scent lingers,
or a quiet pool
along a bank
rainbow and brook trout
the long afternoon waits
to catch bugs and flies . . .

elusive magpies
in distant alfalfa fields
and thin cotton blanketed ghost
a few weak clouds
with false hopes of rain.

12/11/72

the sea
unlike an old man
traveling wind roads
sometimes muddy
upon the sun he rides
skimming lakes
hunting for his peace

9/2/72

My eyes open
and everything
before me dies.

the end
trees blowing in the late afternoon
a thousand sunflower seeds
her heart is broken
and my legs hurt
but like cold water
on my face
a new dawn of collected thoughts
and no more fears . . .

Sitting alone in the cold morning
last night's peach wine blindness
I am lost in a place I know
mountain shadows, hot sun
I am afraid to go home . . .

FOR MY UNCLE JIMMY

Purple breasted robins,
fly over Santana's music
while plastic sun cakes
run for cover under my song.

He gave bear to the soup
and hummingbirds to sixteen
summers and breathed only one
blade of grass on the hill
of sacrifice dying
before my song.

His soul cries
for religion which never
knew a mother, searches
the trees.

A MAN AFTER LUNCH

On the bank
down from me
a man sends
cigarette smoke
into the air.

A leaf
from a nearby
tree
drifted into the
stream where
I stood.

Worms dug deep
as though to escape
the plane crash
killing all its
occupants.

My neighbor runs out
of cigarettes
and I can smell
the flowers on a
gust of new air.

DEER

Should the deer die
in its sleep or the leaves
never turn green,
I couldn't care less.

Leave me among reflections;
let me fall into mud puddles;
don't bother to look back,
for roots don't snag my feet.

Collect the dew
in the morning
and pick a fish
from the stream.

When you go towards the valley,
to the beaver lodges,
tell your lover I never bothered
his traps and from wherever
the sun may fall
I couldn't care.

www.ingramcontent.com/pod-product-compliance
Lightning Source LLC
Chambersburg PA
CBHW051706040426
42446CB00009B/1328